Get to the Airport

Written and illustrated by Maxine Lee-Mackie

Maxim and Lena were going on holiday.

They had to get up and get dressed.
It was still night time.

The street was dark.

Dad said, "We must creep out. Everyone is still asleep."

"Not me!" yelled Lena.

Shhh!

Mum had the biggest bag. Dad groaned when he picked it up.

Maxim had the smallest bag. Lena just had her little teddy.

It started to get light. Maxim was sleeping.
"Are we there yet?" yelled Lena.

Mum turned into the airport car park.

"We are at the airport now," said Dad.

They pulled their bags into the airport but Lena began to sob.

I left my teddy in the car!

They all went back to get the teddy.
"There he is! Silly Lena!" said Dad.

At last, they went to check in the bags.

Dad checked his pockets. Dad checked his bags.

Dad went bright red as he looked for the passports.

Mum pointed to his back pocket. It was the passports!

"There they are! Silly Daddy!" yelled Lena.

Talk about the story

Ask your child these questions:

1 Why did Maxim and Lena have to wake up early?

2 Why did Dad tell everyone to be quiet when they left their house?

3 Who had the biggest bag?

4 Why did Lena start crying at the airport?

5 Have you ever had to get up very early to go somewhere?

6 Have you ever lost something precious to you? Did you find it again?

Can your child retell the story in their own words?